CAGE OF EMOTIONS

Edited by

Andrew Head

First published in Great Britain in 1999 by
POETRY NOW
1-2 Wainman Road, Woodston,
Peterborough, PE2 7BU
Telephone (01733) 230746
Fax (01733) 230751

Copyright Contributors 1999

HB ISBN 0 75430 584 8
SB ISBN 0 75430 585 6

FOREWORD

Although we are a nation of poetry writers we are accused of not reading poetry and not buying poetry books: after many years of listening to the incessant gripes of poetry publishers, I can only assume that the books they publish, in general, are books that most people do not want to read.

Poetry should not be obscure, introverted, and as cryptic as a crossword puzzle: it is the poet's duty to reach out and embrace the world.

The world owes the poet nothing and we should not be expected to dig and delve into a rambling discourse searching for some inner meaning.

The reason we write poetry (and almost all of us do) is because we want to communicate: an ideal; an idea; or a specific feeling. Poetry is as essential in communication, as a letter; a radio; a telephone, and the main criteria for selecting the poems in this anthology is very simple: they communicate.

CONTENTS

RESURGAM

Don't mess with me when I am down
And have no strength to fight,
Don't think that when I'm vulnerable
I don't know wrong from right.

I care not what your status be -
A council clerk or royalty,
I will repay your tyranny
If you should mess with me.

I've been to hell before - and back
I know its nether reaches,
The pain and grief along the track
And what the journey teaches.

Body and mind are mortified
The spirit suffers too,
Until it emerges fortified
To face the world anew.

Don't mess with me when life is grim
And dreams have turned to ashes,
Don't think that I'll forgive the pain
Inflicted by your lashes.

Like a phoenix I'll arise
To blast your scorn into the skies,
You'll long remember how unwise
You were to mess with me.

Mary Rutley

A Child's Home

When I was a child
Unguarded and alone
I used to wander wild
And thought the world my own.

The tall trees on the grass,
Sometimes a few weeds,
Green leaves that lightly pass,
Later the autumn seeds.

Yellow bushes bright
That down the driveway led;
Lilac purple and white,
Roses pink and red.

Fields lay all around
The hedges mounted guard
Where the hawthorn wound
With scent of spikenard.

The ivy-covered walls
That led down to the gate,
Where the slow stream falls
And where the meadows wait.

And then the lonely bay
Where the seaweeds shine.
This shall forever stay,
A magic that is mine.

Jessie Lamont

DECEIVED EYES

Look at my eyes
You'll see two beautiful big brown eyes
Come more closer to my eyes
You'll see two black irises
Go deeper into my eyes
You'll see tears forever
Streaming like a lake
Look into my tears
You'll see my hurt
Feel my pain
My desperation calling for help!
My life sailing away to the unknown
You'll see me clinging
On to precious life
Look at my eyes?

Saima Salim

I'LL BE HERE

I saw her at the window
Watching the children at play,
Knowing that tomorrow is their future
But for her just another day.
'I'll be here'
She'd often say
'Until time takes our love away.'
There from her window
She'd watch the leaves just fall
Knowing that winter time was on the way -
And at night in times of loneliness
At those stars she would stare
Just waiting for one to fall.
The window's dirty now there is an empty chair.
Now on the wind,
As the last leaf of summer is about to fall
I thought I heard her say
'If I had a penny for each star in Heaven tonight
I'd be a millionaire
I'll be here close by you
Until time takes our love away.'

K Lake

SOMETIMES THE SKY GETS TIRED

The sky flashes its frail whispering wisps
of moving sentiment drifting 'cross a tired sky
That feels millions of years of staying up there
Its invisible arms strain to keep up the concept
A large expansive concept that is as
Predictable and unpredictable as the humans it cloaks.
Did it want to run on forever and be blue or white?
Did it plead to be allowed to turn black at night?
Like a black and white photo it can be shades of grey
But fade or curl or held fast in an album 'tis not.

We expect the night-time to turn sky blue black
Save for a silvery glimpse of brave cloud daring to stay
Whilst the rest darkens and daylight is forgotten.
Night light embraced and cradled by dark endlessness.
The dark's twinkling age old lights need no bulb or switch
Wink impishly high above - those naughty golden playful
Dancing five-handed creatures!
Hide and seek in daytime hours, cloud allowed now,
Cotton wool stretched thinly over blue pink blue print.

Whimsical and fluffy and gentle soft floating mists
Became angry and itchy when Earth displeases high blanket.
Let the people see I still exist, I live and breathe!
Pour rain and sleet in gushful torrents, drench them
In my wet power.
Flash thunder bolts in zigzag angular angriness
You'll see and hear me unpredictable and war-like.
You can't fight the might of the aloft with all your
pathetic flimsy umbrellas and passive acceptance
Of a powerful force.
Shout at me, humans, cry, scream and yell!
At least I know then you react to my outpourings
Instead of muttering amongst yourself as to how bad it is.

J Maddock

BLUESED (TO BE SUNG BY BILLIE HOLLIDAY)

Don't know why he hits me
Don't know why he hates me
Don't know why he gets so mad
And I
Don't know what's makin' him so bad

But he's
Not the man I fell for
Who I said I'd go to hell for
Didn't think he would take me there
Or that
All our love would grow so bare

So I
Know I've got to leave him
Because I can't believe him
When he says he really cares
Then he
Does something that really scares me
So I've got to walk away
So I've got to walk away from him.

Chris Birdsall

HALLOWE'EN

The old man in his bed, was
Nearly dead. Alone and ill
He heard the letterbox, children's
Voices, young devils' shrill,
Down the stairs.
The smash and crash -
A decisive bang.
After which tiny feet hoofing
It, down the drive away - and ran.

What was that? - Only the mind
Could reach: out to the impenetrable
Landing-in breach.
When suddenly came a mustard gas
Or so it seemed, like sweaty feet;
Stink bombs a trick or treat.

The old man went at half-past five
Into an oblivious world and died.
And just to think the last hours of his
Life, the dregs: were endured
With the smell of rotten eggs.

David Hazlett

UNTITLED

I drank the brew the wizard gave,
And gazed upon my Earth,
I found what I'd been searching for,
The present from my birth.

The colours that I knew were there,
The whispers of the wise,
That told me that there's more than this,
That there exists a prize.

I saw volcanoes spewing gold
to children who were poor,
Saw lions help a buffalo who'd
fallen to the floor.

All the world was one big smile,
Which always ran in synch,
And everyone helped everyone,
And had the time to think.

Ashley Wilks

ALPHABET POEM

A arrived at the seaside,
B burying my feet in the sand,
C climbed up the rocks,
D discovered crabs in the rock pools,
E entered the sea,
F fishing with my dad
G getting very hot,
H hurried down the prom,
I including people to play,
J jumping in the sand,
K kicking around a ball,
L licking my ice-cream,
M munching on my sandwich,
N nagging at my mum,
O opening a bag of crisps,
P peeling my orange,
Q quarrelling with my sister,
R running on the beach,
S swimming in the sea,
T teasing my dog,
U using my spade to dig the sand,
V visiting the gift shop,
W watching the boats go by,
X exhausted from a fun day,
Y yawning, ready for home,
Z zoomed for the bus home.

Jade McAuley (9)

I'M HAVING A BABY

A mum-to-be not long left school
Has indulged a grown up relationship
Taking no love protection apart from
Anxiety of telling parents or guardian
Seeming very cool.
Looking forward to her baby in this modern age.
Seeing baby on ultra scan machine wants
to know baby's sex male or female at this stage.
Getting support from her family
Considering her new life she does carry
She has much from experience to learn.
But her life has involved younger sister's baby age
So from then she had much to bring to her aid in return.
Making a good mother at times can be very hard,
But with support after novelty
Joy of new baby in her arms.
Needs so many basic needs
Happily England is a welfare state.
So financially their needs will be catered for
An unmarried mother also baby are protected
which is great.
In this day also age unmarried mothers are many
They have jumped house queues have homes of their own.
This seems unfair for many others on housing list of councils
Who have to protect new babies
Many young have so much chance of birth control
Free but just leave it alone.
Will attitudes change most mums be married
Future it will be known.

Victoria Joan Theedam

IT'S THE WAY THAT YOU SAY IT

Shopping with my toddler daughter and son,
Was always fraught, though sometimes fun.
'Can I have?' was my daughter's shopping name,
While my son was of 'I want it' fame.
A simple 'No' would never suffice,
Such an utterance was really not very nice.
It was often followed by tears of lament,
Designed of course to make me relent.
So, 'At Christmas' I would often say,
Or 'Maybe you can have it on your next birthday.'
After weeks of such excuses to avoid the fray,
My son made an observation that could only dismay.
'The thirty-fifth of Wrongtober is what she means,'
'She says that 'cos she doesn't want a scene.'
'But there's no such month and there's no such day.'
'Why of course, never is what she means to say.'

G E Khandelwal

NIGHT DRIVE

Passing, passing, fading, dying,
The twin red lamps of passing cars -
Winking blinking, interweaving,
Glowing, growing, yellow stars.
People coming, people going
In their caul-like metal cans,
Now departing, now halloing,
Controlled clearway, cats' eyes showing,
Following their ordained order,
Driving to their several plans.
People, people, men and women,
Little children strapped in seat -
Faster, faster, through the glooming
Faster than the fastest feet.
Lights are quick, but thought is faster,
Faster still man's body flies
Hurtling with the yellow headlamps,
Only leaving twin red eyes.

Joyce Baith

A RATHER OLD MAN'S POEM

I don't remember much about the 1930s dear,
When Mother coped with seven kids and Dad was into beer.
I do recall that times were hard where money was concerned;
We just got used to hand-me-downs, and somehow never yearned
For luxuries and fol-de-rols and all this fancy gear.
Except for bumps and bruises, we hardly shed a tear.

We had our fun on roller-skates, and when they fell apart,
We used the wheels and salvaged planks and made a sort of cart
That steered with string and went like stink when facing down the hill.
Provided at the wheels stayed on - and we stayed on as well.

There's one dark time that comes to mind in all my looking back -
When Mother scrubbed the kitchen table so that Doctor Mac
Could take my brother's tonsils out and, for an encore, mine.
(She wanted all the dross stripped out before the age of nine).
Poor Doctor McIlhinny went and shot himself next day
And Mother took us all to church and tried to make us pray.
She never really blamed me for the doctor's suicide,
But how I feared that I should be arrested, charged and tried.

I got away with that one, but over all these years
It stays a chilling chapter in my childhood souvenirs.
I'd rather dwell on Dymchurch and our yearly holiday.
Such fever of excitement, such rejoicing on the way.
The sun that woke us daily and shone for all its worth,
And golden sands that reached out to the edges of the Earth.
What more could children wish for in those everlasting days?
Days of blinding happiness; all white - no blacks or greys.
I dare say memory registers just the things it wants to hear.

I don't remember much about the 1930s dear.

James Johnson

SUNRISE

It used to be when the sun would rise
I would turn over and close my eyes.
For who would want to welcome the day
When nothing ever went the right way.
Feelings of anger, resentment, fear
Filled each moment with so many tears.
Days were a nightmare that had no end
So alone with not even a friend.
I used to wonder what would become
Of this man if he didn't run.

I woke up from this horrible dream
My eyes beheld a wonderful scene.
A room full of friends who showed me the way
To face the problems that came each day.
I listened I learned, at last I grew
To share my feelings was something new.
From fear to faith, I turned life around
Smile on my face and feet on the ground.
I now can enjoy greeting each day
Coping with life as it comes my way.

William Price

SNOWFLAKES

I love to watch the snowflakes falling,
Gently to the ground,
Little drops of frozen rain,
That fall without a sound,

The beauty of a snowflake,
So crisp so pure so white,
To watch the snowflakes falling,
Can brighten a cold cold night,

Snowflakes are a thing of beauty,
Forever I wish they would stay,
But sadly when the sun comes out,
They gently melt away.

Sylvia Ranby

WHAT A WONDERFUL SOUND

'Tis sounding within the emerald green forest
What a wonderful sound that fills my heart with rapture
Such a call of wildlife amongst the trees
Oh wonderment in music of the birds
So softly like an orchestra in concerto
Refrains with chorus sweet and low
What a wonderful sound
Rising accompaniment of the birds
Within hiding amongst the spreading branches
Chorusing in harmony nature's choir sings
And throughout the forest music becomes louder
A tumultuous sound amidst the emerald green
What wonder of nature charms my heart with rapture
What a wonderful sound
When sunshine gleams like a stage light upon the scene
Oh sweetest sound of song as the birds sing
Such harmony of wildlife freedom
Amidst the forest's emerald green kingdom
O may every forest be preserved as a sanctuary
And e'er continue a wonderful sound of harmony
What a wonderful sound
'Tis sounding within the emerald green forests.

Margaret Howens

UNFINISHED

Somewhere there's a rainbow
With the colours of my heart.
From the tears that I was crying
When my life was torn apart.
Shackled by my conscience
A prisoner of invaded mind
Intolerable truth cascading by
Images that remain unsigned.
Temptation tears me to pieces
Because I can rarely resist.
Morality gives up the chase
Shakes an enraged fist.
Bad decisions come so easy
In a life so full of delusion
Screaming vultures hover overhead
Patiently waiting for my conclusion.
                    (To be continued)

David J Burke

WEATHER PLEASURE

Hark! Listen to the breeze rustling through the leaves,
With the rays of sun filtering through the trees.
Watch the shadows as they dance on the ground,
Honestly there's so much magic if you only look around!
Just look at the clouds floating like cotton wool up high,
An ever-moving picture, all yours up in the sky.
For even the storm clouds that seem to annoy,
Holds power and strength for all of us to enjoy!

While the rain makes small rivers and trickling waterfalls,
Look at the beautiful colours when oil merges in the pools.
Then there's the droplets that hang onto the last,
With the light catching then it's as if jewels have been cast!
When the glistening frost arrives it paints everything white,
It's as though someone's been busy, secretly throughout the night.
Leaving us with some beautiful mosaics all over the glass,
Has everything been starched just stand on the scrunchy grass!

Then a blanket of fun is sent in the form of snow,
For this is a time for everyone who likes to have their show.
Who has the biggest snowman a competition in the street,
It's a time for adults and children for they all like to compete!
So you see it doesn't really matter, whatever the weather,
For all seasons hold their magic, plus their pleasure.
So learn to enjoy them for they're here for just a short time,
Remember it may be cloudy and cold but the sun will always shine!

Ann Beard

MY WAY

Dear Frank Sinatra
Now that you've gone
Your voice on your records
Will always live on!
Give my love to Matt Monroe
And our lovely Princess Di
Thank you! And all the stars
Already up in the sky!
When you were all here
You made our clouds roll by!

Liz Jones Knapp

DICKENS' DREAM

Running from the ghosts with a face so white,
I thought he could be doing with some rouge
But as he passed close - with expression morose,
I knew it was Ebeneezer Scrooge
He was met by Micawber, that crafty old robber,
who begged him to please spare a penny
I'm very old said Scrooge, and I have no gold,
If I had you wouldn't get any

'Oh don't be so mean it's the Xmas scene - so surely you
can spare a Copperfield - I mean copper'
'Humbug!' He said, 'Get lost or you're dead,' then he hit
him real hard with a chopper.
'Something will turn up, something will turn up'
He kept saying, as he met my pitying glance
And for once he was right, on that eventful night
As along came an ambulance.

The doors opened quick, as they do for the sick
As old Eb' violently shook his fist
So they threw 'Cawb aboard - and away they roared
Driven by Oliver Twist. 'He looks done in' said Tiny Tim -
But seems like a decent old codger
Going over a hump, there was a terrible bump
And there lay the Artful Dodger!
So I woke from the dream, with expression serene
But it soon transformed to a smile,
To think that those greats - for a time were my mates
Made my dream, seem all so worthwhile!

Gordon Rainey

IMAGINE

Imagine that you
Could see into the future
What it has instore for you
Imagine that the oceans
Were grey instead of blue
Imagine that the birds
No longer sing their songs
Imagine that all the trees
Have all long since gone
Imagine all the meadows
Lifeless silent and bare
Imagine all of this
Yet no-one seems to care.

Alan Green

ON THE DOORSTEP

He stands on the doorstep, requesting
Something he really needs.
First thoughts: 'You're a nuisance,'
And 'Why is it *me* who feeds!'
'Why not go to the agencies
Or a charity in town,'
And, as though he knows what I'm thinking,
His face set with a frown:
'I'm your neighbour!'

One day *we* may knock, requesting
Something we really need.
Will *we* be judged as 'a nuisance',
Or will someone lead!
Offering the helping hand
Instead of turning away;
The smile of a good Samaritan;
A welcome display:
'You're my neighbour!'

Denny Rhymer

ARTIFICIAL FLOWERS

Why despise artificial flowers?
When they look so real
And they last forever,
And their petals never drop,
From when you buy them from the shop.

I arrange them so artistically
In dainty little vases,
Red, yellow, blue, pink, and white
Then stand them on our windowsill
They really look a lovely sight.

At times someone comes along the road
Then suddenly stands so still
And admires our flowers
Upon our windowsill.

Amy Barrett

DEFINING LOVE!

A shining light
glimmers so bright,
and seen by the eyes of the blind
True love is found
when you've not searched around
so therefore is genuine and kind.

Your heart won't grow cold
as you begin to get old
It just sends you more of a warning
The things you now feel
soon seem less real
because of past sorrow and mourning.

Catherine Humphreys (15)

SILENCE IS GOLDEN

Silence a rare commodity
In this changing world
It helps you to collect your thoughts
And troubles to unfurl
Of course there's always silent prayer
When you are in a crowd
The pace of life can quicken
Without it being loud
Silence is a pathway to sweet serenity
Sop silence is still golden
And is there for you and me.

Mary Tickle

A SOLDIER'S RETURN

The soldier home for the rest of his days
Be it Beau Geste
Collapse in the heat, weak heartbeat,
A soldier's retreat by golly we were beat,
By an Army elite,
One soldier's return look at the burn
Stop and return,
To home his eyes would roam
The secrets of a soldier is to get bolder
The winter colder, the winter war,
If we knew it well, in a cell,
If time could tell.

John Bain

THE LATE TED HUGHES

Words of sadness and words of sorrow
Things that may make sense tomorrow.
Words of fear and of hate
All that hide one man's fate:
Special secrets of a lost wife
That he held all of his life.
Words large and grand
Some things folk don't understand.
Poems that don't amuse
All in the mind of that Ted Hughes.

A mind on a different plane
Poetry you can't explain.
Work ahead of its time
Words that don't always rhyme.
Words that give the wrong impression
Hiding one man's hidden aggression.
Life's wonder in its repose
The secret pornographic sin exposed.
Books to give the sand man the blues
All in the mind of that Ted Hughes

Poems for the deeper state
Words that some men love to hate.
Pain that racks a body and soul
Words printed to fill a role.
Lines for the soul to prick
Poems some people find sick.
Line after line of useless trash
That the inside of some brain will smash.
Like the blowing of a celestial fuse
All in the mind of the late Ted Hughes.

Colin Allsop

LUCKY THE LEPRECHAUN

The dwarfish light green sprite made his way
through the grass,
some coins had fallen from a pocket while
some man made a pass.

He wheeled the metal underground back to his
workshop cave,
and made himself a brand new knife for which
he had a crave.

Some tools for him to cobble tiny shoes were
next in line,
so he could sell them at a fair to which his
folk incline.

Lucky jumped upon a table carved himself
some cheese,
he'd get a straw draw off some drink filled
himself up with ease.

Beachcombing brings Lucky plenty metals,
gold and wood,
a shellfish lasts him all day long the
shells make baths so good.

Even if they see him he knows they cannot say,
anything to their neighbour or they will be
put away.

This Lucky little leprechaun enjoyed his
happy day,
he never had a thing to buy as men threw things
his way.

Jean Paisley

SOUL MATES

I want to be wrapped around you
Your touch is so good
Tangled in your emotions
Your wish is my command

We are soul mates through and through
Pure soul mates me and you
We are both in control now
You know it's true
I want to be your angel guide you all the way
I want to protect you both night and day
I am your only angel here forever to stay

Hypnotised by every touch
Every touch from you
Destination unknown time will tell
What is to unfold
Travelling the Universe
In a force so great in a world so true
Travellers in time
Touching all the planets along the way
You will always be mine
Until the end of time.

Teresa Farrell

WHAT IF?

What if?
As a child I had been good and obeyed my parents,

What if?
I heeded every stricture and was a paragon,

What if?
I was of good repute and refrained from evil,

What if?
I did to others as I would be done by,

What if?
I gave to the needy with no thought of self,

What if?
I lived a good and blameless life,

What if?
I coveted not my neighbour's wife.

What if?
All these were true,

Would I be able to look myself in the face?

Lak Si

AM I A FOOL TO FEEL THIS WAY?

The rain pounds down on the windowpane,
Am I a fool to feel this way I do?
Darkness fills the cold world outside,
Yet within these walls with you we make our own light,
Roses grow where none have grown before,
Laughter now fills a life lived in a pool of tears,
Your voice brings calm to my storm of emotions,
Somehow you have made my fears melt like snowflakes in the sun,
My inner world is once again filled with warmth and love,
How can one man change my world this way?
Freedom at last from the chains of my past.
By your side I no longer live in the rain and dark.
I hear music where no band plays,
Feel the sun on the stormiest of winter days.
Sometimes my mind turns to my long lost love who lives now in
heaven above,
I can almost see his smiling face, giving blessing to our love,
Who can tell what tomorrow will bring?
Where we will be?
So for now the happiness and love I shall roll in like fresh clover,
The laughter like the morning dew to the new blooming rose,
I shall love you as the birds love the dawn,
Care for you as the bee tends the flowers in bloom
This I shall do for you throughout the weeks, the years,
With joy and love in my heart.
Am I a fool to feel this way?
Gladly I will love you until and beyond the day we are
forced by an unseen hand to part.

Kathy Lunnon

AFRICAN DREAMER

African dreamer.
Silent schemer.
Ride the roads where nobody goes.
Get to your destiny, which always question me.
Have a good life.
From your dear wife.

African dreamer.
Silent schemer.
Pick up the pieces,
which lie beneath us.
Hold them up to the sky,
and wipe your wary eye.
Luck is with us.
Why make a fuss?

African dreamer.
Silent schemer.
Love is like fire,
when you have much to desire.

Go with the flow, that we already know.
You are in my soul, which will never get old.
African dreamer.
Silent schemer.

Now that you have gone.
I shall begin to move on.
You will always be missed.
Sealed with a kiss.

Sharon Rovers

THE GENERATION GAP

Why do some children, not listen,
      To what, old folk, have to say,
Instead, of calling them, 'Old Fogies',
      And saying, 'You've all Had Your Day.'

'Cos the old folk, have experienced, life,
      And gained knowledge, on the way,
So they could share it, with the young ones,
      To prevent them, going astray.

Pensioners, have lived through, all the stages,
      But still remember, their Teenage Years,
And they'd like to help, the youngsters,
      Overcome, their worries, and fears.

So to bridge, the Generation Gap,
      They should share, each other's view,
Because, the Teenagers, will have to realise,
      That they, will grow old, too.

Jean Hendrie

ELGOL

From remote Elgol at the road's end
The view stuns the eye and seeks to send
The viewer into raptures as he stops to gaze
At wild Coruisk and the dramatic Cuillin maze.

The scene so often hid by mist and cloud
Tells little of the drama that time now does shroud
So much here is hidden, until you look
Slowly: carefully you open the closed book.

This is a romantic but cruel land
That demands all if you are to stand
and harvest a crop or haul some fish
Bad weather then on table an empty dish.

From here the Bonnie Prince did flee
To go for ever across the sea
Now ruined cottages dot the hillside
As his followers driven away; exiled.

Today at Elgol buckets of EU money
Try to create a land of milk and honey
New road, new cottages a village hall
A new life; the old hard to recall.

Roger Coates Smith

THE TECHNOLOGICAL RHUMBA

When you're telephone-pestered without apology
It's time to call in some cheap technology.
Here's how to frustrate double glaziers and such -
If you do it right it'll not cost you much.

First you must do what their callers always do
And dial 141 before you start.
Then when you're through they can't get back to you:
That's information the system won't impart.

Now use their 0800 call, it'll cost you nowt at all,
And that done, hold the line and press button three.
Repeat the 0800 number and do the technological rhumba
As you recall the other line, for just 5p.

You must not make a sound as their recording tape turns round,
All it must record is 'engaged'.
Excuses must seem lame as they try to lay the blame,
And their accused staff become enraged.

Of course, for more immediate fun here's what could be done:
Use their live line for your second call
But don't forget to 141 and keep silent till they've gone.
You wouldn't want to spoil your little ball.

It will cost you more money but you'll find it really funny
If you chose two live double glazing lines to connect
But still remember 141 and the silence till they've gone;
After all, *you've* got *your anonymity* to protect.

R L Cooper

THERE WAS LIGHT

When God our Father made His world
He made both night and day
The sun ruled the world by day
His reflection moon, ruled night
Men, in those far-off mists, named time
Saw everything was 'good'
Later, and most certainly now
They are mostly 'misunderstood'
For some turn night into day indoors
by incandescent light!
While we of age seek fine light's warm and cosy glow
Our days, of love and romance with time had to go
Recall we youth ah 'No!' no one ever may
Write of life, and everything, but that crucial day!

Jessie Harper

PAIN

Just to stand on the precipice of despair
To cross that line where no one cares
Sinking lower than darkest Earth
Fearing that you have no worth

For age is external withering
Downward path bodies slithering
Hours that drift like a cloudy sky
Hating sleep for the waking draws nigh

Maybe there's a reason for galloping pain
Is it a test? I beg not again
The sorrow I feel constantly fills like a jug
Each time it is tipped it fills every mug

Shake off this feeling that's a cold damp coat
Know there are many on the edge of the moat
Wanting a kindness to turn them away
To take a step forward to which way they might sway

A kind word or a touch may be all that is said
Dear God know our sorrow show compassion I beg.

Susan Goldsmith

TOMMY'S NOVEMBER

November's here again,
wet and damp and cold
They're selling poppies in the rain
for those so brave so bold.

They died in freezing mud
in fields that weren't their own
Everywhere - noise and blood
Where stench of death was blown.

They were not afraid, they
dared not so to be
For if their fears held sway
The death squad would be ready.

Kipling had it right with his
'Tommy this and Tommy that.'
What a load of tommyrot
He knew the differences between
the fire of bullets from the Hun
and those his mates, had shot.

These they'd surely fire
Before the rising sun
Had lit that blasted wire.
And Tommy's day was done.

Yes, Tommy this and Tommy that
He never had a lot
For if Tommy feared, he knew
He'd bloody well get shot.

So over he went into the sickening gloom
Daring not to think
As his feet jumped to the
boom, boom, boom
and gunpowder's filthy stink

All cannon and guns with bayonets
held forward for the kill.
He didn't know his worth would be
a poppy red, sold, to pay his bill.

He couldn't let his mates down
What would they say at home
His brain awhirl with prayers
He'd never really known.

No, he didn't give his life,
It was taken, that's for sure.
What got him through was hoping
There'd be no more bloody war.

So give me a poppy to put upon
my coat or shirt or dress
To show I'll not forget you won.
Remembering with honour, Never ever less.

W M Francis

THE CALL OF THE SEA

My soul cries out to the call of the sea,
Its gentle ripples calm and placate me,
I must see it, touch it, hear it,
My spirit is renewed as a fire within is lit.

There is a wildness within me which is masked,
As I revel in its moods and bask.
In the sights and sounds of its massive tides,
Huge waves on which the surf rides.

When I feel the spray clinging to my face,
My heart begins to pound and I quicken my pace,
I hear the mighty waves crashing on the shore,
I see this mighty spectacle, could I ask for more?

I am filled with exultation as the wild wind rages,
In its battle with the sea and engages
All its subterfuge to decide who is master,
The fight continues faster and faster.

Suddenly, the wind drops, the sea is still and calm,
Their quarrel can no longer cause alarm,
I've seen, heard and touched, I hear a gentle sigh,
I am at peace, I must return again, or inwardly I die!

Irene Greenall

ARCADES AND ALLEYWAYS

The arcades and alleyways that cross my troubled mind,
and reek of my existence.
Serve to hide my evil past, where scattered souls who put
their trust in me, lie lost and undefended, amongst the heaps
of rotting memories that I have disregarded.
No respect for life or for love.
I lived only for my self advancement.
But now my once able body has turned against me,
My life now under threat.
Called to account for what I cannot answer and will not justify.
What God would invite me into his heaven when my soul is
blacker than an endless night.
What hell would recommend me to its master when I am more
deserved of his crown.
Am I to live my second life suspended between two worlds, no
claim upon my soul,
Or I could find forgiveness for the unforgivable with a love I have
yet to know . . .

Floyd Coggins

COUNTRY LANE

A country lane, stone strewn and gullies by water hewn.
Twisting and narrow, rough like the furrows.
Dog roses cascading, with pink petals strewn
and long green sword all rank and lush,
twisting, winding t'ward village brook.
Where strangers from cars and coaches
stand and stare - and look.
Oh! Country lane, surviving still twisted,
turning, with mane of green, poorer are those
who know you not; have not experienced our half-veiled
wonders or your beauty seen.
Place of solace; Place of peace,
sanctuary, holding forth, your long green isle
yellow hammer, quick of movement;
powder puff of rabbit tail.
Butterflies serenely dance and sunbeams smile.
Drifting smoke of traveller's fire
dappled sunbeams prance and
framed by leaf; the village spire.
Treasury of many wonders;
Holder of natures law.
Each new step; each new glance,
even then this, will offer more.

Clive Cornwall

AT THE SEASIDE

As I run onto the sand.
The crunchy silky sand.
I watch the dog's paddle,
While I make castles out of the sand.
Then I watch the fish gliding peacefully in the sea.
Next I watch a school of fish swimming away from me.
Their slippery scales are like a rainbow passing through the sea.

Carey Donkin (8)

THE P. S. WAVERLEY

With cleaving prow and streaming wake,
Her threshing paddles wheeling.
The gallant Waverley's in view,
Along the Solent steaming.

She's bound to westward through the roads,
Her engines sweetly sighing,
And bravely heads a fresh'ning breeze,
Her pennants briskly flying.

The last fair lady of her kind,
From Scottish waters hailing,
Proclaims through siren blasts her mind,
To long continue sailing.

Albert Hart

WHISPER

Is it only a year since I last heard your voice
sing to me, before the silence that was your choice.
Why then yesterday, floating through my brain
did I hear your distant words echo once again?
Was it a finger of a sea breeze stroking my hair
to make believe you had metamorphosed there
or was it merely the whisper of a gull's wing?

Bees hummed lazily over the cropped clover carpet
hidden by tall-tailed meadow grass, inviolate,
private place where no-one could intrude on my reverie.
As I looked from my cliff top perch above the sea
at Braille-like dots down below, punctuating the creek,
a warm breath seemed to brush my unsuspecting cheek,
or was it merely the whisper of a gull's wing?

Flocks of white fans feathered the pink blue sky
as smiling, chubby cherubs floated by
then puffs of Jupiter's smoking breath blew along,
my small world now a speck of dust beneath this throng.
A shiver tap-danced slowly down my spine,
from far off a melodic cry I could not yet define,
or was it merely the whisper of a gull's wing?

Laughter of toy soldiers stepping along the water's edge
floated up in waves to my barren, lonely ledge.
You were not there, perhaps in retrospect, had never been,
seeing only what I wanted, blind to what I should have seen
my wild imaginings ran riot, convinced me otherwise.
I wonder now if there was a spark of love amidst the lies
or was it merely the whisper of a gull's wing?

Heather Bruyère Watt

POEM TO A MOTHER

You were the first sight, the first image
For a tiny life engulfed in wood,
Staring upwards, afraid and not understanding.
You were there, instantly comforting
With your soft tones tinged with practicalities.
You were there for the first step,
For the first fall,
You were there in times of trouble.
When the sky grew darker than the velvet night-sky
And thunder crashed and rain leapt,
And you were there when the sun shone,
Brighter than any shooting star
You were always there!

And now, you're still there
But the tiny bud has grown
it has bloomed and flowered.
And now, it can stand alone against the rigours of the work
But it hasn't forgotten!

You will always be there.
Long after your candle has been dimmed,
Because you are everything.
I am growing, developing, trying to find my place,
And I forget, I neglect,
I bottle emotions like some fine wine,
But there is no wine sweeter than you,
There is no-one to take your place.
Everything I am, I am because of you,
Everything I own, I owe to you,
Everything I can ever do
I'll do for you . . .

Michael Doherty (13)

FRIEND

Solid, decent and with respect
Unassuming, unpretentious but direct
Pleasant and polished to look your best
You stand with dignity from the rest.

I lifted your lid slowly and took a peek inside
What I saw amazed me and opened my eyes wide
Inside are priceless treasures, you're lined with solid gold
So many precious secrets the world has not been told.

I'm honoured to have met you
And this is really true
To be your friend, I am proud
Glad I took time to look beneath the shroud.

Agnes Jones

ESTHER'S LOVING MEMORY (15TH AUGUST 1998)

Blessed are they that mourn: For they shall be comforted.
Matthew Chapter 5: Verse 4

I would love to take your hand,
To see your gentle smile,
To see you walk the garden path
In your simple country style,
Now I must live with memories,
Memories of gold.
Esther now walks in God's garden,
God's lovely garden above.
All I can hold is her picture in frame of gold,
Signed, *from Esther to Mother with love.*
The pain of a broken heart when a gentle voice is still.
One day we will meet again, in God's heavenly home above.
All I can hold is her picture in frame of gold
Signed, *from Esther to Mother with love.*
Someone betrayed our country,
Tearing many lives apart,
Now I live with memories of gold,
The pain of a broken heart.
One day we will meet again, never more to part.
Now I hold dear Esther's picture,
Smiling face in frame of gold,
Lovingly signed in letters of red,
To Mother from Esther with love.

Frances Gibson

CHANGE!

Here I stand entranced on a russet brown carpet
of leaves driven by shock to a frost filled earth.
The grass glistened like a million diamond rings
sparkling in sunlight
creating crystalline coats.
Trees yielded to nakedness on this mid-October morn
Leaves floated effortlessly down to a ground
not yet prepared for change
there to remain forever trampled on.
Whilst denuded branches mourned their departure
And yearned for Spring
to recycle them . . .
Spring came as usual
But the rain hammered harder.
Flash floods fell from charcoal-leaden skies
But Earth was getting warmer
as the hole in the ozone layer widened.
Change is here to stay!

Judy Studd

SOMETHING MISSING

Love without commitment.
Life without a plan.
Passion in the heart,
Dies like a crumpled flower
In the hand.

M Rossi

ON AND ON

Rusting wrecks run on asphalt highways
Crumbling concrete, towering skyways
People keep rushing here and there
And on and on, to who knows where!

Structural steel spans over sea-ways
Radio waves are pulsing space-ways
Picking up sounds from who knows where
Then on and on into atmosphere!

Tentacles of cable, spread underground
Linking together town after town
Telling the news to people who care
Then on and on to who knows where!

Astronauts fly to far off places
Searching out galaxies for other faces
Hoping to bring more knowledge to share
Then on and on to who knows where . . .

GIG

TREES AND ME!

As we change our looks
Our dark, luxurious locks
For thinning lines
And strands of grey
So trees change too.
Our change is just once
They have an annual display
Of variety, virility and vanity.
At the close of each year
They may turn from green
To every shade of fire
Sparkling with rain
Blazing with sun
Golden as apples.

Alive and yet dying
Ready to end as naked and barren branches.
Then, with spring,
To bud again,
Cool, aloof, distant, the warmth to come
Bursting with blossoms
Rippling with youthful muscles to flex.

Helen Wadley

WISDOM

The capuchin monkey
stared through the mesh,
sad-eyed, old-eyed, and wise.

He did not climb and spring
among the branches, chattering,
as other monkeys did.

He thought. And knowing how the world
was just a cage
robbed him of joy.

He stared at me
(who thought me free) with pity. I cannot
escape that stare.

I wish that I were old enough to know
what he saw where I stood.
And dread the time knowing.

Fred Brown

VIEWS OF DELHI

Coming from the airport through the steaming night,
Seeing the fires flicker through fading trees -
An arclight shadowing the potholed road,
And lightless buildings, huddled each
To each in anonymity,
Glimpsing, as we passed, a trishaw park
Where children slept, dreaming a different dream
There on the harsh, unyielding ground;
Where hopeless beings, left-over lives,
Crouched while the firewater
Mingled with their tears . . .

Then, from my morning window, under the bright sky,
Seeing the neat lawns edged with flowers,
The blue pool, the cool trees' comfortable shade -
(Invisible beyond the wall
The shouts of morning vendors
And the clip-clop horses market bound).
While far above and over all,
I see the black kites wheeling, wheeling . . .

Mary Jameson

NEW SIGHT

I treasure every flower that I see this spring
I memorise each bud that I see grow.
I wish I'd learnt much more from you
Before you had to go.

But when I look at all these things
I think of you again,
And know how much you loved it all
The sun, the snow and rain.

I feel I'm seeing such a lot
For the very first time.
I'm seeing them through your eyes
As well as using mine . . .

J Wendy Dale

HER DREAM

The competition was on - the child entered,
Everyone was excited for her.
She practised and practised
But then she lost
And all hope was gone.

Family tried to comfort her,
But her dream was lost.
But then it didn't matter,
She had found the confidence to enter
Another competition
Soon she won
And all hope was found!

Rachel Henningham (11)

POET IN AUTUMN

Wing by wing I hear the autumn coming.
Silent love in the falling leaves.
An empty boat stands ont he shore.
I am alone but the wind is talking about me.
It says I am a poet without words . . .

Marion Schoeberlein

THE SCOURGE OF NATURE

So once again, the seasons turn
and once again, a lesson learned.
We cannot silence wind and weather
(a mighty force when linked together).
Much needed rain, in summer's heat
relentless falls in vale and street;
The gathering force no boundaries know
highlighting misery with snow
and treasured homes cannot withstand
the fierce erosion of the land.

'Oh, will it never end?' we cry,
as drearily the days go by,
And heavens endless torrents spill
on field and mountain, vale and hill.
Whilst wild winds howl and moan and scream
and mountains make of sea and stream.

And nightly we absorb the scenes
of devastation on our screens.
As much loved homes the floods invade
and those nearby are sore afraid.
For man, - with all his vast resources -
can't stop the waters in their courses.

And yet we wake one day to sun
and feel the storm its course has run;
'A lovely day' we gladly cry
to other people, passing by.
So easy, with our lives intact
for us to overlook the fact
that nature's misery lives on
with no *quick fix* for homes now gone
For treasures lost and carpets soiled
and all the decorations spoiled.

We cannot help, but should keep green
the pain and sorrow we have seen.
And if we're safe and dry, and warm
and haven't suffered in the storm.
Remember those who count the cost
of now replacing what they've lost.
Their cleaning-up has just begun
For their sakes, let us pray for sun!

Joyce Newlin

MAUDLIN STREET

So cold the April wind
Plucking pale blossom from the hopeful trees
I too, am hopeful, long waiting to be here.
Viewing the city, the arc of its fresh day sky.
Daily I hurry uphill passing the populace by.

But now I stop to watch these yearning western skies
So limitless, so pure, open to love and inspiration, I could stare
Perpetually like Keats' carved angels forever eager-eyed;
Stare forgetting, forgotten, at the co-eternal
Sky earth embrace, regardless of time.

Street rooted commuters hasten on
Beneath the great adventure of the morning sky.
Blind to the falling shadow's edge, it gilds from oblivion
Lapsed dusty spires amidst high-shouldered office towers.
So they like me - continue to shuffle on and up
Or scuttle down the hilly town.

S Fairclough

MY DOG!

I have a wonderful, playful pup

L oveable, funny and drinks tea from a cup.
O ver all she's frisky
V elvety soft fur,
E ven though she gets into trouble!

D on't think there'll be any cure
O f her natural craziness
G reat fun for both of us
S o much more exciting
   than a game of chess . . .

Laura Durkin

THROUGH A CHILD'S EYES

I wonder what are their thoughts?
When between tall legs they get caught.
They look up and it's the wrong face
Oh dear! They have lost their base.

Where have mum and dad suddenly gone?
Why are they suddenly all alone?
All around the world's gone weird
As the faces they want - have disappeared!

Then through the mass the wanted face
As mum and dad come through the space.
To find their own cherished one
To gather them close - take them home!

Constance V Chant

BEST FORGOTTEN

People peering, prying, trying, poking, peeking, snooping, sneaking,
Creeping, sticky beaking.
A Nanny state - it's for our own good,
Nanny knows best,
That's understood!

People hiding, overriding, message controlling, news withholding.
Movement checking, vetting, repealing, all concealing.
Number knowing, *they have yours* - TV cameras out of doors.
Records that are never seen, kept on government machines.
Lots of things that you forgot, our minders of the state - have not!
There's tapes and transcripts everywhere,
And it's only done - because they care . . .

Julian Forster

Unemployment And Disability

Signing on - a regular task
In a life with a lack of routine
No job, no cash - just a Giro
Or perhaps a government scheme!

Try applying for this
They say in ways of sort
Before you can do anything
They plonk out a form for income support.

Expansion of skills is an option
Well, who can refuse?
With all the *Eco* gloom possible
What hope is there in the news!

Applications forms, Cvs and interviews
Jobclub, *JIG or ET*
It's still unemployment
Who said that they'll want me?

Don't ask people in Social Services
They'll make the obvious stop
Disabled and unemployed equals
To them a *sheltered workshop*

So please companies and ministers
It's time you stopped to shirk
Look at all the disabled
And give them *respectable work!*

It goes to show how greedy
The bigwigs can be given - a chance
Whilst us - the ordinary people
Are victims of *squeezed finance*

P Edwards

IS ANYBODY LISTENING?

So close, yet so far
I reach for your light
Up in the dark skies
Lights burning bright.

I wish, upon you
As night draws in,
To bring peace and happiness,
And rid the world of its sin.

Up to the dark skies,
I say my prayers,
Is there anyone up there
Who listens . . . and who cares . . .

Sylvia Connor

TO BRITISH VIRGIN-ROSE

(A dedication)

Open for me your right fragrant breast,
Oh! British most beautiful, innocent Rose.
So that I may see your true heart within your chest
Not touched yet by dart of flamboyant Eros!
Let your pretty lips of red petals inhale
The breath of eternal love from my longing lungs.
To make your heart to tremble for a while
In ecstasy of purest, but not of a pain pangs.
Let our passion embrace in forgetfulness of dreams
With our purest and innocent intents.
Bathing in celestial approval of glorious gleams
Just for a second co-mingled with exotic scents.
Let heaven observe my kiss upon your fragrant lips,
And let God join your trembling heart with mine;
Let us forget everything in a mirthful sleep
Oh! British Rose - heavenly divine . . .

Stanislaw Paul Dabrowski-Oakland

THE SPITTING COBRA

The symbol of Satan
A creature of curses
A curve and a curl
Of this scaly sculpture,
Forked finesse with flattened features,
A sunset of colour
Captured in each and every scale,
The snake . . .
Easing quickly through the undergrowth,
Sleekly, slipping, spitting out poison,
Death rides like a highwayman
With a sunken hood
The serpent of Genesis.
Lives on . . .

V J Swandale

THE TWO BONNIES

Bonnie was Bonnie and none can deny,
But who was this other, aloof - not at all spry.
The same ginger colouring, eyes - yellow green
Relaxed lying comfortably and always serene.

Bonnie perpetually hungry, or so he'd pretend,
Till he had your attention, and down you would bend.
Just two spoonfuls, no more, in his dish,
More, more, he would beg, I'm starving -your wish.

But Bonnie No 2 stays tranquil and calm.
In spite of flowers, plant pots, spread-eagled, none came to harm.
But the Bonnie we knew, 'spite treading with care
Plant pots sometimes landed broken - deep in armchair.

There'll be an explanation, I'm sure you'll agree,
If you saw them together, in a twinkling you'd see.
For one with fur coat, eyes bright, whiskers a twirl
The other a flat painted coat in a frame - on the wall.

As like as two peas, perhaps you would say,
But one warm, vibrant and friendly, the other no movement all day.
But maybe the whole of the stories not there
Perhaps when I've wound my way up the stair.

Two Bonnies frolic and dance on the rug.
More food disappearing - Bonnie No 1 looks so smug.
For who are we to know what can be
With such enigmatic felines - as all cats can be . . .

G Wade

FAUN

In the garden the sun blazed,
Wakening her primitive self,
Secret, wicked, wilful.

Heady colours, reds purples,
Vibrant oranges, competed for,
The sweet favours of bees.

Heat touched the garden seat,
Blistering the wood,
Bringing thoughts of love.

She melted like honey,
Into lazy dreams,
Of longing.

Woodland spirits called to her,
Abandoning her hat and shoes,
She sought the woodland path.

In a clearing a strange boy,
Blonde, naked,
Playing on a stringed instrument,
Beautiful as Balder.

Afraid of beauty she ran back,
Thinking him human,
He was the midnight faun.

That night she did not sleep,
All night his hooves beat hard,
On grass outside her window.

Peeping, she saw him horned,
Hoofed, yet half human,
Then eyes met in the long summer.

Kathleen Scatchard

GOOSE FAIR

The occasion is always looked forward to,
By all the children who visit there,
They do not like to miss the fair.
Even mums and dads like to go.
Roundabouts and swings
Coconuts and things
A good time is had by all
Like going to the ball . . .

A Ausher

THE MARCHING SOLDIER

The castle stands so strong, against its foes.
A soldier marches to and fro.
His battle's over for the day, Oh! How he wishes
That there would be no more battles for him to fight,
So that his weary bones could be laid to rest.
The castle - it's in ruins, but still he marches on!
Since no man has learnt to live in peace with his fellow man.
So still he marches on - over the battlements so strong.
Will he ever receive his liberty?
I hope he will for a hundred years.
He's marched on over the battlements so strong
At night he would like to give up the fight,
And let the peace reign once more over land and sea.
That's up to you and me.
If the soldier is to be given his liberty!

Amelia Campbell

MEMORIES FADE

My eyes fill with water,
and a gentle tear runs down my face,
watching you leave my life.
Forever!

I keep remembering the time we spent together,
we walked hand in hand,
with a bond that we thought . . .
couldn't be broken!

Memories fade as time changes,
New memories never re-made,
only gradually forgotten,
and never returned to my heart!

Lindsay Hedgeley

UNTITLED

Sitting here wondering what to do,
Cannot decide - can you?
Could go walking - no not that!
I could play with my fat cat.
How about swimming, the waters cold,
No! No way! I'm not that bold.
Walking, running lots of choice.
Football match, I'll lose my voice.
All this thinking has made me tire,
I'll put the kettle on instead.
Warm myself beside the fire,
Make a cuppa and go to bed . . .

Karen Westmoreland

FOREVER

My naked flesh, so still in the night
Darkness caresses my soul.
My aching heart bleeds for the light
For sorrow has took its toll.

My love he sleeps in another land
In a yearning cry, I weep out
To hear his voice . . . but no words . . .no reply
To soothe my heart and doubt.

Thy sweet sound, once spoken to enlighten
Thy heart was so happy it beamed
But alas it's gone and I'm frightened
Was it real or have I just dreamed!

My heart will love him forever,
My soft skin can still feel his touch.
These lips still taste the magic
In your arms the warmth was so much.

Goodbye, my love, I still love you.
But my life is in the here and the now
It's true I was kissed by an angel
Will we meet again?
In the next here and now . . .

Delline D Clark

ALIEN INTERVIEW

To place an extraterrestrial visitor before us on a live TV screen,
Stimulates our finite minds to focus on a truly remarkable scene.
he lurches forward against the glazed barrier, in failing distress,
Telepathically communicating with remarkable ideas to profess.

The interview, conducted by a chosen few, casts an awry spell.
Fearless death approaches as life transcends to an awaiting cell.
Deserted on this planet by lost companions, holds no latent fear.
Death is a mere transformation and signifies new rebirth is near.

His lifestyle clings to darkest night and our brightness is a bind.
The lenses protecting his eyes forbid us to search into his mind.
His world is a dark world where light is a catalyst of some pain.
Like a blind person he finds earth's anchor a restrictive domain.

Yet, his intelligence is light years beyond us, difficult to impart.
We tear his broken ship apart, delve into the secrets of its heart.
We use captured technology to conjure up a new *stealth* plane.
Secrets plunge to hidden chambers, entombed from light again.

Fortified army camps portray the obvious cover-up to deceive.
New technology must be born from human minds we believe.
It wouldn't be right to publish ideas from a distant outer space.
All would lose confidence in the supremacy of the human race!

T Burke

JUDGEMENT

This is my hour of darkness, my time to bleed
All these questions unanswered as I fall on bended knee
What did I do wrong, I scream and please - *forgive me!*

What you did was wrong but that doesn't make it right
You knew your crime, long before its act
You just couldn't stop, no ledge to grab?
Unconscious but fully aware
So stand up straight whilst I take aim
Get ready sinner - *here comes the pain!*

But I'm just a man, not a God
You gave me this pedestal just to push me off
And as I fall, you just stand and watch
With that grin on your face, it's just too much.
Will I land on my feet or flat on my face
Or is it all *just down to fate?*

Fall and break, make no mistake
For when you hit the ground, you'll continue down,
Into the gutter and down the drain.
When you come to rest, it will be at my feet
And from that moment all you'll be *is a fading memory!*

All I've done is what you asked
You pulled the strings and made me dance
You said *trust me, take a chance!*
And like a fool I took your hand, now I'm a condemned man
With no faith to guide me left with only hate to consume me.
As my candle starts to go out, I shall stand strong and proud
Never giving up or giving in
This is one fight you'll never win!

Andrew Jones

THE PHEASANT

One day as I lay hiding,
Beside a lonely ditch
I saw a gunman coming nigh,
Himself, his gun and his bitch.

There was I in radiant colours,
So terrified could be.
Thinking that this animal of a man
Could bring an end to me.

As it is in my nature to deceive,
I lay as still could be.
The gunman urging his dog along
Touching its tail and his knee.

As the dog drew closer, I burst into flight,
The gunman to the left, I flew to the right.
I was lucky once more but the thought of that fear,
This dreadful deed so unnecessary.

Tim O'Sullivan

POEMS IN MY POCKET

Poems in my pocket,
Poems in the hall,
Some are on the ceiling,
Most are on the wall.
Everywhere are there poems,
They're only to be found,
Take a thought - pick it up,
Then turn it all around.
The words are formed, one by one,
Just as it comes, it can't be wrong,
Your mind is now in poetic tune.
Now carry on, you will finish real soon.
Near to the end, now finish in style,
Writing a poem, to make everyone smile . . .

Rie Kidd

UNTITLED

The world floats
In frozen time
The girl in the window
Slips down
Drinks her wine . . .

The moon sparkles
Street lights shine
But the flame flickers
And breaks the line
Of hope
The dove falls . . .

Round her now
Raindrops down
She looks up
But the sky is dry . . .

The bottle is empty
The window broke
Her world shattered
Silently she chokes
On the pain . . .

She tries to stop
The rain falling
Falling from her eyes . . .

Ruth-Naomi

MEMORIES

Blessings asked for during family prayers
Automatically mother would sing up the stairs
'Everybody in and chained down!'

One at the bottom, one at the head
Two sisters slept in a single bed, where
A huge china piddle pot rested
Decked with Cambridge blue flowers.

Junior state school; parrot style teaching
The order of the day. So was heavy discipline
Not one of us had anything to say,
We were there to learn, not to think.

Gym class; girls, while lying flat on your backs
Raise your right leg high without strain
Bring down your leg immediately
We can't play this one again
You are not properly equipped!

Saturday morning pictures:
Having earned twopence for entry to the flea pit's screen
Where body beautiful could be seen,
Rescuing his Jane from a waterfall
Introducing us to the classical crawl
Thrilling stuff, Tarzan alias Johnny Weissmuller.

We merrily played hop-scotch, marbles, leap-frog, skipping
And many more games in our street,
Dealing cards under the gas-lit lamp post
I never saw anyone cheat.

This childhood I would have hated to miss
This temporary case where ignorance was bliss.

Respect and loving kindness,
Kept the wretched grown-up's level.
String in the door, nothing to steal
All in the same boat, that was for real . . .

Eileen Barker

DEATH

Don't be sad now
Do not cry
I am only sleeping
I did not die

Feel the breeze upon your face
Or see the leaves in their Autumn chase
Please don't waste time just asking why
For I am here with you
I did not die

Suddenly see my sickly face
I tried against time so quickly to race
I lost the battle but won the war
I will always be with you just as before

M I Salter

Sarah's Secret Garden

If I could walk in Sarah's mind, I know what I would find,
A place where talent and intelligence, are so magically entwined.
Her mind is like a secret garden, with much hidden behind its walls,
With a sweetness that is like the sound of a robin as it calls.

Like a garden on a summer's day, her mind can be so full of life,
A place with a beauty all of its own, within a world blighted
                              by strife.
Like a garden on a moonlit night, her mind can be serene
                              and enchanted,
I hope that the dreams she dares to dream, will one-by-one
                              be granted.

I have seen the radiance of her mind, more than I could dare to hope,
I have been getting to know her more and more, and have observed
                              her mental scope.

Sarah's life has often been blighted, by yet another black cloud,
Damaged by people repeatedly, the light to her soul often blocked
                              by a shroud.
The storms have continued to lash her, more than the Highlands
                              could withstand,
Her trust in others has been eroded, like waves hitting a castle made
                              of sand.
And people have sometimes told her, that there is nothing special about
                              her mind,
But if only they bothered to look for the key, a secret garden they
                              would find.

D Pestridge

THE SOMME

Here in the trenches we all lie;
We know tomorrow we will die
When over the top we must go
And face the bullets of the foe.

Here on the battlefield of the Somme
In our minds are memories of home,
Of friends and neighbours and loved ones;
We will really miss them when we've gone.

When our bones find a resting place
And we have gone through Heaven's gate,
Will all the people living back home
Never forget us dying on the Somme?

Today the battlefield will be red
With blood that flows from the dead;
For all of us who here lie asleep
I pray to God our souls to keep . . .

Francis Allen

NO LOVE FOR COUNTRY

With the country's money troubles
through recession and falling shares.
It has got some people worried
those who are millionaires!

I heard a professor talking
about the rich and the elite.
He said they had money in foreign banks
preparing to take flight.

Like rats who left the sinking ship
when things got out of hand,
So the rich folk do the same
with money at their command.

The workers are left to fight alone
through poverty and pain.
They know now that they've been conned
by those millionaires - again.

It is time we had far better laws
to give the poor protection.
So they do not suffer much
through those wealthy folk's defection . .

Lachlan Taylor

QUIET COMPANY

Ah! I hear the rain a whispering
in the wind, pattering on the glass
echoing voices speaking in the distance
ghostly footsteps on the grass . . .

Quiet inside the room I sit in
only my little bird chewing on his seed
no-one would think in my quiet composure
that company is my pressing need . . .

Lynne Heather West

LAST POST

(Dedicated to my brother Frank Whitlock, standard bearer,
Royal Engineers, Woolwich)

The poppies of Flanders are blooming
To remember the dead of the wars.
In the distance a bugler playing
And he's told you his stories before.
So wear your poppy with pride,
When you honour the dead of the wars.
For those who gave up their lives
For they could not give us more.
So we will always remember them
And let us never ever forget . . .

P Jarvis

SUSSEX - OLD AND NEW!

Rolling downs and
chalky cliffs -
pebbled beaches
framing summer seas.
Fields of poppies
and waving corn.
Sussex barns
and cottage thatched.

Idle ponies
and cattle mixed -
Lazy days on Beachy Head,
looking down on
lighthouse small.
Millions of magpies
everywhere.
Where do they come from
I'd like to know?

Piles of tyres -
Black plastic too
covering hay bales,
or so I'm told!
Roads of traffic
and peaceful lanes -
Shady avenues
of latticed trees
and golf courses galore.

Country towns
with Saxon spires,
Country towns
with terraced houses
and twittens leading
to the church.

Seaside towns
with royal connections -
seaside towns
with nudist beaches
and elegant piers
marching over the waves . . .

Constance E Findlay

FULL CIRCLE

My father used to say
'One day lad, you'll be old like me.
Then you'll know'
Know what? I thought.
The secret of life! No, that would be exciting
and my father didn't look excited.
He looked old and disappointed
resentful and angry
because his limbs were stiff
because he'd lost his youth.
'Come on! I'd say. You can do it Dad
It's all in the mind!'

Yesterday my son came to visit me.
It was a tiresome business.
He wanted to take me out in the wheelchair.
'No son! I said, it's too cold, too difficult.
I'm too much of a nuisance.'
But he wouldn't listen to me!
'You'll enjoy it, he said you'll see.
It's all in the mind.'
And I heard myself saying -
'You don't understand, son.
One day you'll be old like me!'

Valerie Thame

AT TIMES

Tremors of what I should have done,
hit me with dull, blunted resonance.
All hope lost in an eyeblink of sorrow,
carried on with unknown emotion.
Toward the misty truth of tomorrow.

So men have distorted truth and form,
this form yearns for a manlike God,
to forgive him, to forget him -
Thus allowing him to be a *fool*
in wasted entirety.

Thus, hoping for a future to rival the past
is like sailing a boat,
with no rudder, no mast.
the rudder controls the direction of fate.
The mast full of holes.
The breeze comes too late . . .

S E Glover

THIS? . . .WAS ME

I've tread the path of life,
My journey's nearly o'er.
And soon the day will come,
When I shall be no more.

I search my mind to find,
If a useful life I've led!
Or one so full of selfishness,
Or greed perhaps instead!

I have no wealth to leave behind,
No property do I own.
Nothing that has substance,
Just me and me alone.

But do I leave a memory,
That others now might see!
And say with such strong certainty,
This then here? . . .Was me.

M Muirhead

THE FEAR OF DROWNING

In a rush of realisation
someone's head exploded
on the bus today
no-one alluded to the fact
in fact
the scenery flashed by
as dreamily as ever
an entertainment
for hum-drum minds . . .

Swimming in this new sensitivity
but completely unaware
she'd had her first fix.
Reality burned away in her brain.
Like some strange narcotic . . .

She tried to comprehend
but could not comprehend
so let herself float
slowly
out of control . . .

Caught in the current
and faced with new fears
she tried to account for lost years
and the fear of drowning
as her whole life
flashed before her eyes . . .

Gary Austin

ROSE

Looking into my garden, and what do I see?
The budding of a flower.
Its characteristics are guided by the bee,
For they change by the hour.
Dewdrops from the night has helped the flower to flourish.
Warmth from the morning sun does help the flower to nourish.
Sweet is the smell, so memorable,
A problem everyone knows,
Thorns that make it hard to cut
That majestic flower - *the rose . . .*

Jeffrey E Herbert

LUNAR RAINBOW

Made by the moon
And not by the sun
I saw it.
(I had read that you were lucky
to see one in a lifetime
so I was indeed fortunate.)
The sky was inky black
Like a darkened screen
Over the city
And my back was to a brightly shining moon.
The colours of the spectrum were sharp
And well defined and awe inspiring.
It led to contemplation:
Were there stellar rainbows I wondered?
Why were the colours always in the same sequence?
Did the Master of the Universe
Who created light and then refracted it
Rejoice at such a spectacle
Of his invention?
When the colours dissolved
Where went the colours
From whence they sprang
Back into nothingness!
Though transient it had a glory of its own
The Author of the lily and the rose
Made it too.
Did it have a message, I wondered?
I am still wondering.
But how glad I am to have witnessed it . . .

R T James

HAWTHORN

Changing in dress
From the red berries of
Winter's surround,
- To a summer edition -
Of a flowing floral gown.

Thorns - sharp and erect,
Worn on each and every bough,
Give warning to those tempted,
That access will not be allowed.

Only those bearing feathers,
Or having the agility of a squirrel's climbing speed,
Will ever have revealed - the secrets,
That under its boughs - hide beneath.

Providing the comfort of a safe haven -
- To wild birds - a nesting place,
And to other less fortunate, unable
To share its company.
- The beauty of viewing -
An upright floral wreath.

In tribute - and lasting memory
- To one other -
Who also wore a crown of thorns
Known as *the Prince of Peace* . . .

Bakewell Burt

ME AND MY TOURETTES

What have I done?
Why pick me!
Have I done something wrong?
Or was it just meant to be!
People laugh
But they don't understand
Please mum!
I can't go through this on my own
I need some help
Give me a hand!
It seems like a nightmare
Or maybe a dream . . .
Sometimes its good
And sometimes its mean.
But I know, no matter what.
My friends will stand by me,
Even in the worst of times,
(Hopefully) there they will be.
I hate it when I twitch, swear or I spit,
But it's a matter of life
So I guess I'll have to live with it.
At the moment
I haven't got that many friends
But in later life
I'll have more I'm sure.
But I suppose it depends.
So people out there with Tourettes
Don't be scared
I'm sure you'll be fine
In fact . . . that's a bet!

Katie Barnett (14)

THE NEED TO BE ALONE . . .

Sometimes the pressure can be too much
and you're stressed out to the bone.
Its when in times like this as such,
you need to be alone.
For a sympathetic ear can be idle chat,
and could well be your undoing,
but in a private habitat.
You can cry out your anger and rue-ing
Friends can be great, when troubles mass,
and you go out for a jar or two.
But if the answer is not at the bottom of a glass,
then your only friend is you.
Sometimes we mix with top brass types,
and think that on water we walk,
But when they speak to us like gutter-snipes,
then to ourselves we need to talk.
For only we know what we need and want,
and of all we have loved and hated,
Thus it is through our personal knowledge font,
that the problem is eradicated.

Because it's hard in life to be a winner
If you don't explore your own self-inner,
Understand on what your feelings are based
That way you won't end up two-faced!

John Norman-Daley

SOOTY AND SWEEP

I have two cats called Sooty and Sweep.
They are a mischievous pair.
They always try to trip me up
when I'm walking up the stairs.

They always come into my bedroom
and start pulling at my feet.
That's their way of telling me
they are ready for something to eat.

They have a funny habit of sitting in the bathroom sink.
They wait patiently for the tap to drip
then they get a drink.

They don't like going outside
They lie and sleep all day
And if they do go out
They're never far away.

They're very much house cats
and never do they roam.
I know that Sooty and Sweep
are content just being at home . . .

A Whyte

CANDLELIGHT

A candlelight flickers
Soft lighting, a warm glow.
The symbol, eye-catching, beckoning
Cutting through darkness, uncertainties
A touch of hope, a clear pathway
World within a shroud
Beauty, even in solitude
Silent and strong
Aspirations?
Perhaps necessity, perhaps majesty
Tools of a worker
Movement that's slow
But indications cry *proceed!*
Obstacles grow near, time to cope
Even tunnels see the light of day
Complications? Avoid being stagnant
Beyond this we are proud
Beyond strife we are safe, and know
Our hopes will have their say
Beauty, beyond travesties
Aspirations proceeding the abyss
World without a shroud
For when the candlelight flickers
It's time to go . . .

Kofi Oduro-A

FEAR OF THE DARK

In the darkness something moves,
By muted moonlight, silhouetted,
Returning shadows of my sins,
All unintentional and regretted.
Terror flies on soundless wings
Across the room, just out of vision,
Clawing at my naked soul
With horrifying, neat precision.
Each slight, each hurt, I have delivered.
Now flurries back, as if to haunt me.
Like fleeting spirits, my regrets
Encircle me, and how they taunt me.
Crushing blackness pounds my temples.
My breath is ragged in my throat.
I cower 'neath the crumpled bedclothes
Blind panic knows no antidote.
I look for light towards my window.
To ease the dread I have endured,
But there shines forth no sweet salvation.
The glowing moon, by clouds obscured.
No subtle gleam of moon or starlight.
Glimmers hope to quell my fear.
I know that hell is surely empty,
Because my demons are all here . . .

J Clarke

FOR THOSE IN PERIL ON THE SEA

They searched the boats all night for life.
Many a man had lost his wife
Who was the mother of his child.
The Atlantic was cold, the Atlantic was wild.
Three classes lived within the ship,
Which eventually did dip
Its whole self into the waters.
Sending sons and husbands, wives and daughters
To their death, some slowly, some quick.
Some were fortunate to be picked up
By lifeboats tied together.
Many didn't survive in the freezing weather
Conditions near the iceberg they had hit.
The unsinkable ship
Titanic's maiden voyage and that was it . . .

Evelyn Burr

SIMPLE THINGS . . .

It's the simple things
The man who can always make me laugh,
Listening to a heart rending ballad,
And looking at an old photograph.
Having a long and luxurious bath.
Those snowy white different formations
Seen drifting high up in the sky.
Admiring an artist's creation,
Enjoying a home made mince pie.

It's the simple things
A little child laughing, splashing around in puddles,
And when he, or she
Climbs upon your knee
Wanting a kiss, and lots of cuddles.

It's the simple things
Like I just can't reach far enough
To bend down and touch my toes.
But I can smell that lovely fragrance
Scenting the air from a beautiful rose.
A person I know passing me by.
While out walking my dog on the lead
Saying *hello,* with a wink in his eye
Giving a helping hand to someone in need.

It's the simple things
Waking up in the morning, feeling refreshed,
That one particular moment of happiness
A good friend talking on my telephone line
Saying; *Goodnight and God Bless* . . .

Joan Taylor

WALKIES!

Come furry friend let's rock and roll,
For it's time for beach patrol.
We'll walk the same stretch of shoreline,
That smells of seaweed and of brine,
And you can savour all those smells,
And I will crunch across the shells.
Collecting those that catch my eye,
The sea, a mirror of the sky.
Once silver grey now cobalt blue,
Making every day a different view

When you were mine . . .

As artists search for form and line,
As poets try to make things rhyme.
I hunger for that long lost time
When you were mine . . .

Was it part of some great design?
That just when things were going fine,
The fates conspire and combine,
To take what's mine . . .

When was the start of loves decline!
The loss of lustre, loss of shine
Those days of roses and of wine,
When you were mine . . .

John Smurthwaite

BURNING HOPE

A tiny match, a flickering flame,
I strike the match to start a game.

A once darkened room is given some light,
To me it looks astonishingly bright.

The flickering flame, the burning light,
Supplying some energy to help me fight.

The empty room is like my mind,
A cure for my illness I wish to find.

That tiny match; A *once* flickering flame,
Suddenly blows out - stopping my game.

That burning match, shining so bright,
Offered me nothing but a glimpse of light.

Alone in darkness I now remain
To helplessly fight my mind in pain.

Tracey Wheeler

KING MAKER

back to the dell
alive on hunters green
better to be seen
alive than mortally dead
in battle or contest
knights the many knights
did gather for battle
in a big attack
and that was that
warwick fell he died
he was king maker
while he did live
no he paid for
his high social life
no man no man
only the dim memory
of the angry past
that is with us
even today with hate
with the non memory
of what is right
remembering only the wrong
on hunters green there
you were able to
hunt the royal deer
as you were entitled
anyone else it was
a death ride
to the one mortuary gate
before the one burial

Richard Clewlow

A Call In The Night

The whistling wind, the roaring sea
  the lifeboat crew sleep uneasily.
The Robert Edgar standing by
  alone and ready for the cry.

Alas the rockets make their untimely call
  a yacht is in trouble during a midnight squall.
Her crew at the peril of the sea
  their only hope comes hastily.

As the lifeboat men battle the sea
  life seems so precious - not just to you and me.
But to all those people who brave the sea
  their valour goes on to eternity.

N C Grenfell

In The Name Of Progress

My granny had a prefab
with plenty of cupboard space
Flying ducks hung on the wall
that always came in threes

My granny was a French polisher
that spoke with a Scottish accent
Had plastic grapes in her fruit bowl
from Woolworth's finest vineyards

A good western was on the telly
so grandpa was in heaven today
He lit up one of his Woodbine stubs
and sat engrossed puffing away

They were kept in a dish on the mantelpiece
granny hated them with a passion
Yet when he rode off into the sunset
they became her most treasured possession

Then we heard a rumour
the prefabs were coming down
The council gave granny a cardboard house
near the shops in town

It had a sign said *help*
right outside the door
A pull cord in every room
and heating under the floor

Soaring electricity bills
came to her address
And stifled granny's budget
in the name of progress

Heather Kirkpatrick

THE GESTURE AND REPLY TO 'THE GESTURE'

You, halt in shadow, poised above me, near
So close, breathing each other's breath, intent,
You tilt your head as if in wonderment
And tuck your tresses in behind one ear.
No other gesture, action or expression
So clearly manifests yourself alone
In person, thoroughly, right to the bone
In one swift flick of elegant compression.
So my heart lurches, wheels and starts to hammer
And my head swims as if with vertigo
To be confronted with - I scarcely know -
A creature of such awesome grace and glamour.
In honour of such loveliness complete
I'd take my heart and lay it at your feet.

Reply to 'The Gesture'

I love to hear those fine words you express
Of me professing to be elegant,
If only, but for you I try to show my gainly side,
They say allure comes from within,
Thank God, for I would hate to pose a false image.
You, my love, I've stared at, for oh so long.
And now I get a chance to look beyond, to see inside;
I like what I can see;
Tenderness, a need to please
Look no further my love.

Enid Withey-Taylor & Fred Cairns

FULL CIRCLE

Orange sashes flutter
In the ill wind blowing through
And red hands clutch the hilts
Of bloodied blades that hatred drew

Flames still lick the sky
And clouds of smoke blot out the sun
As someone pulls the trigger
On another loaded gun

Fatal words are spat
Upon the crowds who dare protest
A Unionist agenda
That sees Irishmen oppressed

A burning rubber tyre
Turns full circle in the road
With Northern Ireland's fragile peace
Once more set to explode

Kim Montia

THE MARVELS OF TIME

Days will always come,
And days will always go,
Just as the sun will always shine,
And the wind will always blow.

But if we wanted time to move,
We'd be wrapped up in sorrow,
Because there is one thing for sure,
We will never reach tomorrow.

Then there is something else, I wish to know,
Could someone make it clear?
Why is it that, forever more,
Today is always here?

And I'm sure there's someone out there,
Who can clear up all my woes,
And also tell me, why it is,
That yesterday never goes.

Marvyn Attwell

NIGHT GARDEN

Autumn came by night
my thoughts like leaves, scattered
and as I walk through my mind,
I kick them from underfoot.
I can't help feeling
that I haven't quite arrived,
I feel tired, yet I can't sleep.
The leaves keep falling.

You are a tree in my mind,
alongside other trees,
some smaller, and some larger
each memory is a leaf
which you shed, to remind me.
They all do it.
The forest of the mind has no evergreens.
And now as winter enters,
all the trees are bare.

Lee Baxter

A B Original - Lamentations

A B Original walked his land with a simple childlike grace,
untouched, unspoken, unsullied, by any other race.
He had his time of dreaming, his time to sit and wait,
And in his childlike innocence, knew nothing of his fate.

He walked the land from sunrise until the sun dipped red,
His only seat, a blackened rock, a willow tree his bed.
The Mother Earth sustained him from the cradle to the grave,
He counted no man enemy and he counted no man slave.

The 'dreamtime' is reflected in his dark and brooding eyes,
A million years of 'dreaming' lived out 'neath cloudless skies,
What magic did his Fathers know? What mountains did they climb?
The answer to the riddles lay buried in the 'dreaming time'.

We took away his heritage, we took away his beloved land,
And all that A B ever knew is buried in the sand.
I would that I could go back in time, about a million years,
To see him in his 'dreaming' and share his hopes and fears.

For now we see the remnant of his former splendid glory,
And only hear a whisper of his past and glorious story.
Our Fathers came before us, and raped his land, his Mother,
How could they do what they had done, to him they call a Brother.

They skinned alive the black men and sent them to damnation,
And on a quiet moonlit night you hear their lamentation,
For all that they held sacred as they loved and walked their land,
Is washed away by the tide of time, - like footprints in the sand.

T J Guy

A DYING FALL

The performance opens in a rainbow of colours
Autumn enters, serene and wistful
Gracefully touching the glorious oak
she turns his leaves deep copper and red
Her lucid breath on the silver maple
ripens silvery points into brilliant shades
of crimson, orange and yellow

This Prima Donna
pirouetting around her stage
Weaves amongst the Corp de Ballet
Now trees of glorious colours
Gold, bronze, yellow
and beetroot pink

Yet backstage
a solitary leaf
Like a lost soul waiting in the wings
dangles limply from a twisted branch
Quivering in the gentle breeze
it appears to the onlooker like
the hand of an old man
Weather-beaten and gnarled
Severed by a slicing wind
it falls
dead
to a waiting earth

Others, still dancing on stage
not yet ready to bow out
Vibrate in harmony with the musical breeze
Their wet leaves glistening in the
Autumn sunlight

Suddenly, the wind like music
rises to a crescendo
Quickening the pace
whirling and twirling the dancers who
struggle to keep on pointe

But too late

The cymbals clash, the drums roll and
the dancers fall with the curtain
Autumn's colourful choreography is no more
Only the scuffing of feet through the
dying leaves can be heard
The performance is over

Jennifer Polledri

THE SNOW QUEEN

Snow-white pines pierce dark green skies,
Where bright stars shine like points of steel.
The Snow Queen comes, with dazzling furs;
The whirling snowflakes twist and wheel

Around her lovely form. Her furs
Irradiate the northern night;
The white silk turban that she wears
Holds one great ruby, blazing bright.

At the edge of the town, where the pine woods begin,
There's a sweet icy perfume, distinctively hers;
The last street lamp shines through the eddying flakes;
There are diamonds of frost at the edge of her furs.

Warm snowdrifts, the rugs in her glittering sledge,
Where she lures me with kisses like peppermint creams;
Transfixed by her eyes as we speed through the skies,
I experience love that's found only in dreams.

Edward Francis

WE'RE OFF TO THE PARK

We're off to the park,
For a bit of a lark,
I think we'll start on the slide.
We'll whizz very fast,
I won't be the last
Or take the skin off my hide.

We'll swing on the swings
And big rubber rings.
We'll point our toes to the sun.
The roundabout calls,
I hope no-one falls,
The hippos are on the run!

The climbing frame shudders,
The see-saw judders,
The park keeper comes to see.
You hippos are rough,
Enough is enough
You'd better go home for tea!

Phillipa Haines (10)

ILLUMINATION

Colours,
So pretty, yet strong and smooth and limp.
The leaves,
They glare at me through my window,
And the trees,
A shower of gold, a cluster of fingers grabbing at the sky,
Another, upright and sturdy; that white bark always looked my way,
It knew me before I did.

Man, flying across the sky,
Looking closer, can see his evidence, that's his bird circling the sky, his
Evolution. Looking up,
Half-lit blue, a bowl wide - hiding
Behind the houses, below me, beside me, on my right, my left
Everywhere, a bowl of sky. So
Green, yellow, red, brown. Our garden.

Shapes,
Now in front, on my sill (too short to hold everything)
Green beauty,
The leaves
Sitting in their miniature forest with different
Dimensions,
A blade of variegated green,
Spades calling to the sun, that it might save itself from . . .
Matches, bullets, jaws, fingers, tongues, a flower of needles,
My garden.

... And as the sun drowns,
Tweaks of man's modern bonfires light the bowl's edge,
Here and there . . . *tweak* . . . *tweak* . . . *tweak,*
They break the Stillness.

Salvatore La Monica

HAPPINESS INHIBITED

Our eyes met across a crowded room - I have memories of that dance.
Was it to be the start of a new experience, could it be a new romance.
And then a second look in my direction made my poor heart flutter.
Then when at last I had the courage to speak, I could only stutter.
Years have gone by and the remote affair that did not get off
the ground.
Has had to remain a fantasy, and yet there's a feeling that judgement
then was sound.
We meet again, and both agree, that there was a spark that we both had
to deny.
For there were commitments to be respected, and we found we
couldn't lie.
We are now both free, and although a little older, enjoy a friendship
with a conscience that's clear.
Happiness we all deserve and will be there if we hurt no-one and our
love is sincere.

Reg Morris